HANDBOOK

Published under licence by Welbeck Publishing
© 2021 Welbeck Publishing,
20 Mortimer Street, London W1T 3JW
ISBN 978-1-7831-2543-2
1 3 5 7 9 10 8 6 4 2
Printed in Spain

MIX
Paper from responsible sources
FSC® C009279
www.fsc.org

The UEFA and EURO 2020 words, the UEFA EURO 2020 Logo and Mascot and the UEFA European Football Championship Trophy are protected by trademarks and/or copyright of UEFA. All rights reserved.

Writer: Kevin Pettman
Design: RockJaw Creative
Editor: Suhel Ahmed
Managing art editor: Matt Drew
Senior picture researcher: Paul Langan
Production: Nicola Davey

PICTURE CREDITS: The publishers would like to thank the following sources for their kind permission to reproduce the pictures in this book.

Getty Images: /Aitor Alcalde: 39R; /Lars Baron: 11TL; /Clive Brunskill: 8; /Jean Catuffe: 21BL; /Denis Charlet/AFP: 24TL; /Reinaldo Coddou H./UEFA: 33C, 40; /Fabrice Coffrini/AFP: 20C, 32C; /Thomas Eisenhuth/UEFA: 33TC; /Franck Fife/AFP: 7BC, 37R; /Julian Finney: 12BR; /Bruno Fonseca/Brazil Photo Press/LatinContent: 24BL; /Stu Forster/Allsport: 22BL; /Louisa Gouliamaki/AFP: 20R; /Laurence Griffiths: 9, 19BL; /Vladimir Grigorev/iStock: 15L; /Valery Hache/AFP: 22TR; /Matthias Hangst: 4, 12L, 35L; /Alexander Hassenstein/Bongarts: 17R; /Mike Hewitt: 19T; /Hollandfoto/iStock: 15BR; /Boris Horvat/AFP: 23TR; /Philippe Huguen/AFP: 28; /Catherine Ivill: 33TR; /Yorick Jansens/AFP: 39L; /Jasper Juinen: 7BR; /Christopher Lee/UEFA: 16UP C; /Virginie Lefour/AFP: 29BL; /Bryn Lennon: 33B6; /Matthew Lewis/UEFA: 17L; /Alex Livesey: 26, 33B4; /Thomas Lohnes/UEFA: 14BR; /Denis Lovrovic/AFP: 32L; / Jure Makovec/AFP: 21TR; /Cesar Manso/AFP: 21BR; /Pierre-Philippe Marcou/AFP: 38; /Clive Mason: 21TC, 34; /Daniel Mihailescu/AFP: 37L; /Mimadeo/iStock: 16B; /Alex Morton/UEFA: 16T; /Dean Mouhtaropoulous: 23B; /Dan Mullan: 33L; /Octavio Passos/UEFA: 18T, 18C; /Pascal Pavani/AFP: 13; /Valerio Pennincino/UEFA: 29TR; /Ryan Pierse: 24BR; /Paul Popper/Popperfoto: 27; /Popperfoto: 7BL; /Adam Pretty/Bongarts: 41L; /Olivier Prevosto/Icon Sport: 21BC; /Gary M Prior: 33B2; /Professional Sport/Popperfoto: 25L, 33B3; /Tullio Puglia/UEFA: 14BL; /David Ramos: 25B; /Michael Regan: 19BR, 30, 32R; /Andreas Rentz/Bongarts: 33B5; /Martin Rose/Bongarts: 25TR; /Mark Runnacles: 16LOW C; /Lukas Schulze/UEFA: 29TL; /Johannes Simon/UEFA: 21TL; /Boris Streubel/Bongarts: 18B; /Lukasz Szelag/AFP: 35R; /TF-Images: 41R; / John Thys/AFP: 29BR, 36; /Claudio Villa: 11BR, 33B1; /Darren Walsh/Chelsea FC: 10; /Ian Walton: 6

Panoramic: /Gwendoline Le Goff: 5
Sportsfile: /Brendon Moran/UEFA: 20L
UEFA: 17B; /Boris Streubel: 15R

Every effort has been made to acknowledge correctly and contact the source and/or copyright holder of each picture any unintentional errors or omissions will be corrected in future editions of this book.

We constantly update and maintain historical records pertaining to the UEFA European Football Championship, and additional UEFA competitions, always aiming for 100% accuracy. Occasionally, however, new facts are brought to light and they may have repercussions on the accuracy of the information here disclosed. Therefore, should you find any discrepancies in this information, we would like to offer our apologies and we would welcome your comments.

The publisher has taken every reasonable step to ensure the accuracy of the facts contained herein at the time of going to press, but can take no responsibility for any incorrect information arising from changes that may take place after this point. For the latest information, please visit www.uefa.com/uefaeuro-2020.

OFFICIAL LICENSED PRODUCT
UEFA EURO 2020

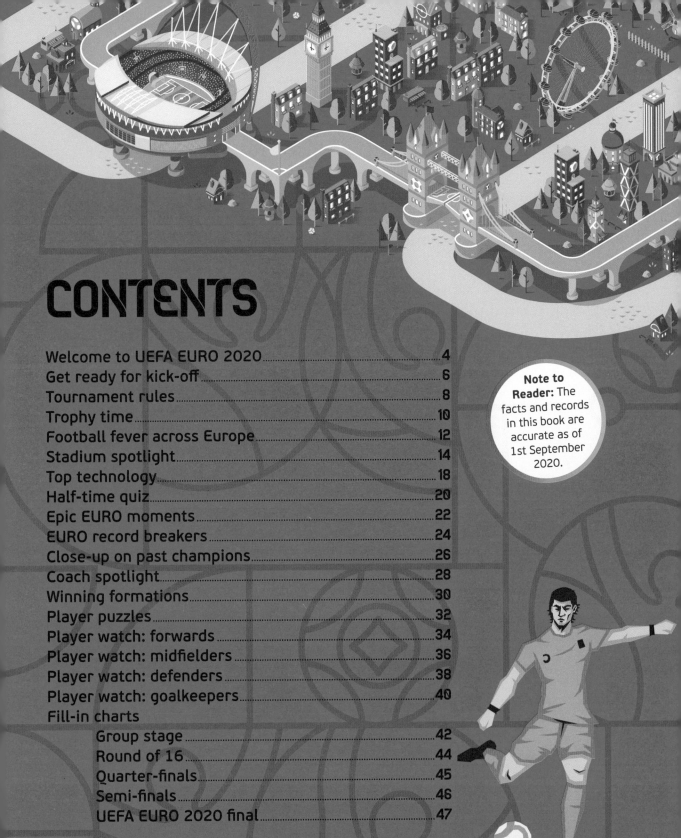

CONTENTS

Note to Reader: The facts and records in this book are accurate as of 1st September 2020.

WELCOME TO UEFA EURO 2020!

The UEFA EURO 2020 football festival in the summer of 2021*
will be the most incredible sporting tournament in Europe
ever. The competition is special for many reasons and, luckily,
everything you need to know is in your Handbook! It is packed
with top team and star player profiles, epic facts, cool quizzes
and exciting pictures that take you closer to the action. There
is even a results chart to fill in as you follow the games.

WHAT IS UEFA?

The Union of European Football Associations (UEFA) is a group
that organises football tournaments and governs the sport in
Europe. Created in Switzerland in 1954, UEFA now has 55 nation
members. The UEFA European Championship is held every four
years and is the biggest international event UEFA looks after.

The Portuguese
team celebrate
after their victory
over France at
EURO 2016.

WHERE IS IT?

UEFA EURO 2020 is being played right across Europe. There are 12 host cities in 12 countries. These include Amsterdam (Netherlands), Copenhagen (Denmark), London (England) and Munich (Germany). Turn to pages 12–17 to find out more about each of the host venues.

Turn to pages 12–17 to find out more about each of the host venues.

HOST CITIES
1. Amsterdam (NED)
2. Baku (AZE)
3. Bilbao (ESP)
4. Bucharest (ROM)
5. Budapest (HUN)
6. Copenhagen (DEN)
7. Dublin (IRL)
8. Glasgow (SCO)
9. London (ENG)
10. Munich (GER)
11. Rome (ITA)
12. St Petersburg (RUS)

WHEN IS IT?

The competition kicks off on 11 June at the Olimpico in Rome – the Italian capital. The 24 teams competing will play a total of 51 matches, including group and knockout games. Wembley Stadium, London, will stage the final on 11 July.

* UEFA EURO 2020 was postponed until 2021 due to the global outbreak of COVID-19 in 2020. The tournament in 2021 will still be identified as EURO 2020.

WHY IS UEFA EURO 2020 SPECIAL?

To celebrate the competition's 60th anniversary (reached in 2020), UEFA is throwing an extra special party! For the first time ever, UEFA is holding the tournament in 12 different European countries. This will allow fans to enjoy the action right across the continent!

Fans enjoy the atmosphere before the EURO 2016 final match kicks off.

GET READY FOR KICK-OFF!

The countdown is on – 11 June sees the UEFA EURO 2020 party get underway! After battling through the dramatic qualifying stage, which began in March 2019, the teams now have their big chance to win the Henri Delaunay Cup. Portugal, France, Spain, Italy, Germany and Greece have all played in the final in the last 20 years, but who will contend the final in 2021?

NUMBER CRUNCH

With 51 matches to be played across 12 countries, there will be at least 4,590 minutes of awesome football for fans to enjoy. EURO 2020 features 24 teams battling to become European champions. Each team has a squad of 23 players, which means 552 international stars will be showcasing their skills and going for glory!

CELEBRATIONS FOR 60

By holding the EURO 2020 games in multiple countries across Europe to mark the tournament's 60th anniversary, UEFA will reach out to supporters right across the continent It is the first time UEFA is hosting the competition like this, so do not miss a minute of this unique and spectacular experience.

England's Joleon Lescott scoring a header in the EURO 2012 group game against France.

SHARP-SHOOTING SKILLZY

Skillzy is the official EURO 2020 mascot. You will see a lot of this football-mad youngster during the tournament. He will be at every match, alongside his freestyle-footballing friends, as part of the mascot teams on the pitch before kick-off. Do you know how Skillzy became the official mascot? Well Skillzy was enjoying a kickabout in a car park with his friends one day when he accidentally kicked the ball through the window of a nearby office. The office also happened to be the audition room for the mascot role. When Skillzy went in to get the ball back, he showed off his street-style skills, which the judges loved so much they gave him the job!

WINNING GOALS

Each picture shows a star player scoring the winning goal in a EURO final, but can you match each image to the correct description?

A Angelos Charisteas scores the winning goal for Greece against Portugal.

B Fernando Torres finds the net as Spain beat Italy.

C David Trezeguet hits the winner when France defeated Italy.

Your answer ▶

The answers are on page 48.

TOURNAMENT RULES

The 24 teams in UEFA EURO 2020 have battled hard to earn their places in the competition. This time, the hosts did not automatically win a place. Instead, between March and November 2019, all 55 sides played home and away qualifying matches against others from one of ten groups (featuring five or six teams) they were drawn into. The top two teams qualified from each group, taking the first 20 spots. A series of play-offs in October and November 2020 decided which teams won the other four places.

GROUP STAGE

Six groups (A to F) of four teams play each other. This means that during this phase each country plays three matches. The top two teams in each group, plus the four third-placed countries with the highest points go through to the next stage. Once the group stage games have all been played, you can fill in the tables on pages 42–43.

ROUND OF 16

This round marks the start of the knockout games. Who the 16 teams play in this phase depends on their final positions during the group stages (see pages 44–45 to find out more). The winner from each of the eight matches progresses to the quarter-finals while the loser exits the competition. If scores are tied after 90 minutes, there will be 30 minutes of extra time, and if that fails to separate the two sides, a penalty shoot-out follows.

Belgium's Marouane Fellaini takes on Italy's defence at EURO 2016.

QUARTER-FINALS

The quarter-final matches are being played on 2 and 3 July at venues in the cities of St Petersburg (Russia), Munich (Germany), Baku (Azerbaijan) and Rome (Italy). These games are super exciting, as teams tend to play attacking football in their bid to reach the semi-finals. At EURO 2016, France scored five goals inside 60 minutes in their quarter-final match against Iceland!

SEMI-FINALS

With the four teams just one win away from booking their place in the final, nerves are bound to be fraying in the two semi-final matches at EURO 2020! London's

Antoine Griezmann scores during France's 2-0 win over Germany in the semi-final of EURO 2016.

Wembley Stadium is staging both fixtures. In recent tournaments, players such as France's Antoine Griezmann, Portugal's Cristiano Ronaldo and Italy's Mario Balotelli have become EURO heroes by netting the winning goal in their semi-final match!

THE FINAL

The match to decide Europe's national champion kicks off on 11 July at Wembley Stadium. The two semi-final winners from 6 and 7 July go head to head, hoping they can clinch glory without the drama of extra time or the dreaded penalty shoot-outs.

SKILLZY SAYS

Spain are the only team to score four goals in a EURO final, beating Italy 4-0 in 2012.

JUST 'FOUR' FUN

Four goals were scored in each of these EURO finals matches, but did each match finish 4-0, 3-1 or 2-2? Write the correct score by each one.

Wales ☐ - ☐ **Belgium** EURO 2016, quarter-final

Czech Republic ☐ - ☐ **Croatia** EURO 2016, Group D

Spain ☐ - ☐ **Rep of Ireland** EURO 2012, Group C

The answers are on page 48.

TROPHY TIME

Fantastic team and individual prizes are up for grabs at EURO 2020. Any one of these awards would make an awesome display in a trophy cabinet.

HENRI DELAUNAY CUP
Since 1960 the Henri Delaunay Cup has been awarded to every European champion, and EURO 2020 will be no different. The trophy was updated in 2008 and now weighs 8kg and is 60cm tall.

TOP SCORER AWARD
The top scorer at EURO 2020 will win the Alipay Top Scorer award. France striker Antoine Griezmann were top scorers with six goals at EURO 2016. Fernando Torres and David Villa (Spain) and Milan Baroš (Czech Republic) have also been leading scorers between 2004 and 2012.

Spain's Fernando Torres poses for a photo after receiving the EURO 2012 Golden Boot award.

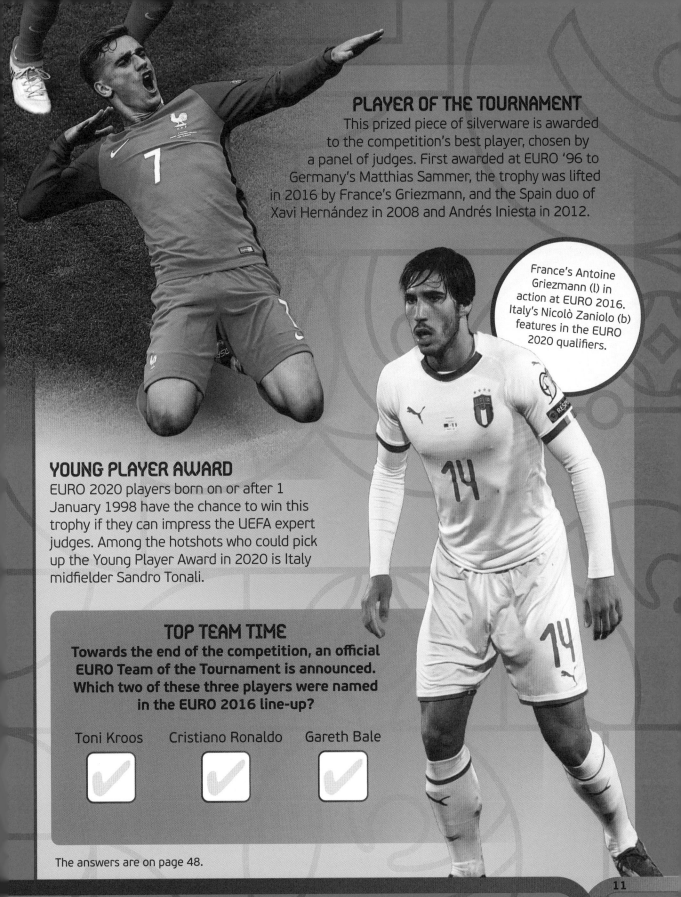

PLAYER OF THE TOURNAMENT

This prized piece of silverware is awarded to the competition's best player, chosen by a panel of judges. First awarded at EURO '96 to Germany's Matthias Sammer, the trophy was lifted in 2016 by France's Griezmann, and the Spain duo of Xavi Hernández in 2008 and Andrés Iniesta in 2012.

France's Antoine Griezmann (l) in action at EURO 2016. Italy's Nicolò Zaniolo (b) features in the EURO 2020 qualifiers.

YOUNG PLAYER AWARD

EURO 2020 players born on or after 1 January 1998 have the chance to win this trophy if they can impress the UEFA expert judges. Among the hotshots who could pick up the Young Player Award in 2020 is Italy midfielder Sandro Tonali.

TOP TEAM TIME

Towards the end of the competition, an official EURO Team of the Tournament is announced. Which two of these three players were named in the EURO 2016 line-up?

Toni Kroos   Cristiano Ronaldo   Gareth Bale

☑   ☑   ☑

The answers are on page 48.

FOOTBALL FEVER ACROSS EUROPE

The 12 countries hosting the finals in 2021 are football-loving nations. England, Germany and Italy have among the most passionate fans, and few play the game more beautifully than Spain and the Netherlands, making these nations perfect for staging this year's special competition.

England fans celebrate during the group match between England and Wales in EURO 2016.

EPIC ENGLAND

England has a special place in the history of football. After all, the first rules (laws) of the game were created in London in 1863. The England team reached the semi-final of EURO '96, when they were tournament hosts, and also won the 1966 FIFA World Cup final against West Germany at the old Wembley Stadium.

NOISY NETHERLANDS

In their bright orange costumes, fans of the Netherlands bring colour, fun, energy and huge smiles to the tournament. Their happiest moment came in 1988 when they watched their side crowned European champions. Could the 2021 side give their supporters something new to cheer about?

Dutch fan proudly wears his team's colours during EURO 2012.

SLICK SPAIN

The style of football Spain play is admired throughout the world. *La Roja*, as the team is fondly nicknamed, have won the European Championship three times. This success has also been repeated at club level, where legendary sides Real Madrid and Barcelona have won the UEFA Champions League multiple times.

GLORIOUS GERMANY

Most would agree that Germany is one of the best footballing nations on the planet. They won the trophy in their first ever European Championship in 1972 (as West Germany), and have featured in every tournament since. They are also four-time winners of the FIFA World Cup. Germany will stage the EURO finals in 2024.

Spain supporters celebrate their team's victory against the Czech Republic at EURO 2016.

HOST WATCH
Draw a circle around the other eight nations that are hosting EURO 2020 games.

Italy

Northern Ireland

Denmark

France

Russia

Scotland

Portugal

Hungary

Rep. of Ireland

Turkey

Romania

Azerbaijan

The answers are on page 48.

STADIUM SPOTLIGHT

It is time to check out the 12 super stadiums hosting the group and knockout games. From brand new state-of-the-art grounds to the older and iconic football venues, these stadiums will showcase Europe's best international teams and players!

OLIMPICO IN ROME

Country: Italy
City: Rome
Capacity: 68,000
EURO 2020 matches: 3 x Group A,
    1 x quarter-final

Did you know? The Olimpico in Rome first staged football games in 1953 and is home to rival clubs Lazio and Roma. It also hosted the 1968 European Championship. All eyes will be on the Italian capital where the tournament begins on Friday 11 June!

BAKU OLYMPIC STADIUM

Country: Azerbaijan
City: Baku
Capacity: 69,000
EURO 2020 matches:
    3 x Group A, 1 x quarter-final

Did you know? The Baku Olympic Stadium is the tournament's easternmost ground, located about 4,400km from Dublin, which is the competition's westernmost venue. Baku staged the UEFA Europa League final in 2019.

SAINT PETERSBURG STADIUM
Country: Russia
City: Saint Petersburg
Capacity: 61,000
EURO 2020 matches:
   3 x Group B, 1 x quarter-final

Did you know? This arena is designed to look like a spaceship that has landed on the shores by the Gulf of Finland, making it among the most spectacular looking stadiums in Europe! The venue staged seven FIFA World Cup fixtures in 2018.

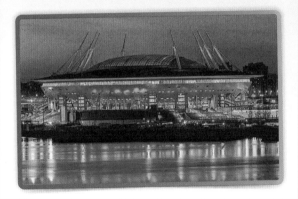

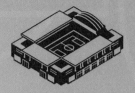

PARKEN STADIUM
Country: Denmark
City: Copenhagen
Capacity: 38,000
EURO 2020 matches: 3 x group B,
   1 x round of 16

Did you know? This is the largest football arena in Denmark and stands on the site of the original ground, Idraetsparken, which was built in 1911. It is the smallest of all the venues featuring at EURO 2020.

JOHAN CRUIJFF ARENA
Country: Netherlands
City: Amsterdam
Capacity: 54,000
EURO 2020 matches: 3 x Group C,
   1 x round of 16

Did you know? Built in 1996, this state-of-the-art stadium was the first in Europe to feature a sliding roof. It was officially renamed the Johan Cruijff ArenA in 2018 in memory of the legendary Netherlands and Ajax superstar.

NATIONAL ARENA BUCHAREST

Country: Romania **City:** Bucharest
Capacity: 54,000
EURO 2020 matches: 3 x Group C,
1 x round of 16

Did you know? Bucharest's National Arena, which has an impressive sliding roof, opened in 2011. Just a year later it hosted the UEFA Europa League final between Atlético Madrid and Athletic Bilbao.

WEMBLEY STADIUM

Country: England **City:** London
Capacity: 90,000
EURO 2020 matches: 3 x Group D,
1 x round of 16, 2 x semi-finals, final

Did you know? Wembley Stadium was redeveloped from the original ground, built in 1923, and reopened in 2007. Since then, more than 21 million visitors have visited the venue and gazed at the majestic arch spanning over the pitch!

HAMPDEN PARK

Country: Scotland **City:** Glasgow
Capacity: 51,000
EURO 2020 matches: 3 x Group D,
1 x round of 16

Did you know? This famous ground used to be the world's largest from 1903 to 1950 before the capacity was reduced to meet safety regulations. In fact, in 1937, nearly 150,000 fans packed into the stadium to watch Scotland play England.

SAN MAMÉS STADIUM

Country: Spain
City: Bilbao
Capacity: 53,000
EURO 2020 matches: 3 x Group E,
1 x round of 16

Did you know? The San Mamés Stadium will literally light up EURO 2020, as its exterior will be illuminated once evening falls! The new stadium opened in 2013 and was also used for the 2018 European Rugby Challenge Cup final.

DUBLIN ARENA

Country: Republic of Ireland
City: Dublin
Capacity: 51,000
EURO 2020 matches: 3 x Group E,
   1 x round of 16

Did you know? The Republic of Ireland's national stadium replaced their Lansdowne Road ground in 2011. Buoyed by their fans, the country has enjoyed big wins over teams like Germany, USA, Poland and Uruguay at their new home.

FOOTBALL ARENA MUNICH

Country: Germany
City: Munich
Capacity: 70,000
EURO 2020 matches: 3 x Group F,
   1 x quarter-final

Did you know? Bayern Munich's home ground was built in time for the 2006 FIFA World Cup and it has also staged the 2012 UEFA Champions League final. This eye-catching arena is fitted with more than 300,000 LED lights that can light up its entire façade in 16 million different colours!

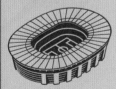

PUSKÁS ARENA

Country: Hungary
City: Budapest
Capacity: 68,000
EURO 2020 matches:
   3 x Group F,
   1 x round of 16

Did you know? This epic stadium is named after Ferenc Puskás, Hungary's most celebrated player. Puskás won three European Cups and five La Liga titles with Real Madrid in the 1950s and '60s.

TOP TECHNOLOGY

The match referee has a tough and very important job in charge of UEFA EURO 2020 games. Luckily he has some helpful technology to help him make quick and correct decisions on the pitch.

VAR

The Video Assistant Referee (VAR) system has been a major piece of technology introduced to the game. The technology, monitored by four video assistant referees, alerts the referee when there has been a clear error on big decisions such as goals, penalties and red cards. The referee can then choose to review video footage of the incident on a screen at the side of the pitch and, if necessary, correct the decision.

Having featured at the last men's and women's FIFA World Cup competitions, as well as the UEFA Champions League and UEFA Europa League in 2018/19, VAR has become a vital aid to ensure correct decisions are made in a game.

GOAL LINE DECISIONS

The referee can refer to goal-line technology (GLT) to know whether the whole ball has crossed the goal line before awarding the goal. A video system in the goalposts checks whether the ball has crossed over the line and sends a signal to a device on the referee's wrist. GLT is useful in situations where there is a goalmouth scramble or when the ball bounces onto the line from the bar or post.

The referee's wrist device flashes "GOAL" when the whole ball crosses the line.

FOAM TECHNOLOGY

All match referees at EURO 2020 will be carrying a small can of foam on their waist belt. The clever 'vanishing spray' is used to mark the position that a free-kick must be taken from, or where the opposition must stand when a free-kick is taken. The foam disappears after a minute or so.

PICK A CARD

Is the referee showing a red or yellow card at these EURO 2016 games?

France
v
Republic of Ireland

Portugal
v
Wales

The answers are on page 48.

HALF-TIME QUIZ

You better be ready to switch your footy brain on, because it is time to tackle the EURO 2020 half-time quiz! Write the answer in the space provided for each question.

WHICH KIT?
Can you name the European nations these footballers play for, even though they are not playing in their usual kit colours?

1 .... 2 .... 3 ....

CODE CRACKER
The name of a famous European football nation has been written in a special code. Read the code breaker to work out what country it is.

A B C D E F G H I J K L M
N O P Q R S T U V W X Y Z

Q P S U V H B M

☐ ☐ ☐ ☐ ☐ ☐ ☐ ☐

The answers are on page 48.

CODE BREAKER: Referring to the alphabet, write the letter that comes before each letter shown here and you will reveal the country.

EYE KNOW
The camera has zoomed in on three different goal scorers. Can you identify who the players are?

1 ....   2 ....   3 ....

....

KIDDING AROUND
Can you name these EURO 2020 star players from pictures of them in their younger days?

1 ....   2 ....   3 ....

YEAR WE GO
Name the year each of these EURO moments took place.

Cristiano Ronaldo scored his first goal at the EUROs

England lost to Italy on penalties.

Manuel Neuer kept four clean sheets in his first four games.

EPIC EURO MOMENTS

Sixty years of the UEFA European Championship have produced some magical moments. From worthy winners to glorious goals and individual performances, here are five of the very best over the years.

PORTUGAL'S PRIZE

Portugal were shocked to lose the EURO 2004 final on home ground to Greece. They finally claimed their first major international prize 12 years later by beating France in the 2016 final. The victory was extra sweet as France were the hosts and tournament favourites throughout the competition.

Portugal's celebrations begin after they win EURO for the first time in 2016.

WEMBLEY WONDER GOAL

England fans have not had much to cheer about at previous EUROs, but 1996 was a bit different. The Three Lions stormed to the semi-finals before losing to Germany. During the group stage, midfielder Paul Gascoigne scored a stunning volley against rivals Scotland at Wembley Stadium to help them top Group A.

England's Paul Gascoigne scores a stunning goal against Scotland in EURO '96.

GOLDEN GLORY

At EURO '96, the final was won with a very famous goal. Germany striker Oliver Bierhoff scored a sudden-death winner in extra time. Known as a 'golden goal', it was the first of its kind in men's international football. Germany's moment of glory meant heartache for the Czech Republic.

Germany's Oliver Bierhoff launches the golden goal shot in the EURO '96 final.

DOUBLE DELIGHT

Spain is the only nation to have won back-to-back European Championships, in 2008 and 2012. In the 2012 final, they swept Italy aside 4-0. Spain led 2-0 at half-time and then added two late goals to secure the trophy. At the time, Spain were also the reigning FIFA World Cup champions after their triumph in 2010.

PERFECT PANENKA

The 1976 final of the European Championship produced one of the most mega moments in the competition's history. In a penalty shoot-out, Czechoslovakia's Antonin Panenka chipped a cool penalty down the centre of the goal to beat West Germany. That style of penalty became known as a 'Panenka' and is still one of the most stylish ways to convert a spot kick.

SPOT THE BALL

In which square is the 'actual' ball from this picture of a EURO 2020 qualifying match?

The answer is on page 48.

EURO RECORD BREAKERS

The stats, facts and achievements in this section mark some of the record highs at previous European Championships. From great goalscorers to young stars, talented teams and super skippers, take a look back at the records set during the competition's dazzling history.

NET-BUSTING GERMANY

In the history of European Championships, Germany (and as West Germany) have scored the most goals. 'Die Mannschaft' as the team is nicknamed, have netted 72 goals in the 12 competitions they have played between 1972 and 2016.

GOAL CRAZY

A record 108 goals were scored at EURO 2016. The fewest number of goals scored was at the 1968 finals, with just seven, but only five games took place that year.

Austria's Ivica Vastić celebrates after scoring against Poland at EURO 2008.

YOUNG STAR

At EURO 2016, Portugal's Renato Sanches set a new record as the youngest player to appear in the final against France. He was just 18 years and 328 days old.

Teen sensation Renato Sanches lines up a shot against Poland at EURO 2016.

OLDEST GOALSCORER

Ivica Vastić claims the prize as the oldest player to have scored in the EURO finals. In 2008, the Austrian netted against Poland at the age of 38 years and 257 days.

SUPER SIX

The Netherlands is the only nation to have scored six goals in a EURO finals match. In 2000 they beat Yugoslavia 6-1 in their quarter-final match.

Russia's Dmitri Kirichenko scores after just 67 second against Greece at EURO 2004.

SPEEDY STRIKE

The quickest ever goal at a European Championship was scored by Russia's Dmitri Kirichenko. Against Greece in 2004, he hit the net after only 67 seconds on the clock.

England players upset after suffering defeat at EURO 1996.

COLOSSAL CAPTAIN

Italy goalkeeper Gianluigi Buffon has worn the captain's armband in more EURO finals games than any other player. He captained the side for a total of 13 games at EURO 2008, 2012 and 2016.

UNLUCKY ENGLAND

The Three Lions hold the unwanted record of playing in the most European Championships without appearing in the final. Between 1968 and 2016, England played in nine EURO finals tournaments in total.

SPOT THE DIFFERENCE

Can you find the five differences between these images of Spain v Sweden in this EURO 2020 qualifying match?

The answers are on page 48.

CLOSE-UP ON PAST CHAMPIONS

It is time to take a closer look at every nation that has lifted the Henri Delaunay Cup. From the first tournament in 1960 to the most recent in 2016, these ten top nations have all claimed the biggest prize in European international football.

USSR

Winners: 1960
The nation that is now represented by Russia, the USSR, beat Yugoslavia 2-1 in the first ever EURO finals, which were held in France. The USSR were also runners-up in 1964, 1972 and 1988.

ITALY

Winners: 1968
The 1968 tournament was unique, featuring the only EURO final to go to a replay. Italy and Yugoslavia drew 1-1 after extra time in the final, and Italy won the replay 2-0 two days later in Rome.

SPAIN

Winners: 1964, 2008, 2012
Spain were the strongest team in 2012 and 2008, winning those finals 4-0 against Italy and 1-0 against Germany. Their first final success came in just the second EURO finals of 1964. They beat the USSR 2-1 at the Santiago Bernabéu Stadium in Madrid.

WEST GERMANY/GERMANY

Winners: 1972, 1980, 1996
Along with Spain, the Germans have claimed Europe's top football prize three times. West Germany picked up the trophy by beating the USSR in 1972 and Belgium in 1980. In 1996, a reunified Germany beat Czech Republic 2-1, thanks to a golden goal scored by Oliver Bierhoff.

The Spanish team hold the trophy following their victory at EURO 2008.

SIEMPRE CON NOSOTROS

CZECHOSLOVAKIA

Winners: 1976

A strong Czechoslovakian team, playing in their first final, were confident of beating reigning champions West Germany in Yugoslavia. The match went to penalties and needed the ice-cool shoot-out skills of Antonin Panenka (see page 23) for the Czechs to pull off a mighty win.

NETHERLANDS

Winners: 1988

Fans of the Netherlands will never forget the team's classy victory at the 1988 tournament. Stars like Ruud Gullit, Ronald Koeman and Frank Rijkaard led them to the final, where they beat the USSR 2-0, with striker Marco van Basten blasting an incredible volley to seal the win.

GREECE

Winners: 2004

A well-drilled Greece team surprised the world by winning EURO 2004. They beat hosts Portugal 2-1 in the opening game and then won the final 1-0, also against Portugal. Angelos Charisteas headed the winning goal.

Dutch legend Gullit celebrates his goal in the final of EURO 1988.

FRANCE

Winners: 1984, 2000

Led by their goalscoring captain Michel Platini, France stormed to the 1984 title on home soil in Paris. They beat Spain 2-0 in the final. *Les Bleus* also won EURO 2000 with a dramatic victory against Italy.

DENMARK

Winners: 1992

Denmark only entered the tournament at late notice but shocked everyone by beating France, Netherlands and then Germany in the final to take the trophy. Brian Laudrup, Peter Schmeichel, John Jensen and Lars Olsen were some of Denmark's key players.

PORTUGAL

Winners: 2016

After the disappointment of losing in the EURO 2004 final, Portugal were finally crowned the European champions 12 years later. Striker Éder became a hero for the Portuguese with his winning goal in extra time.

SHOOT-OUT SCORE

Only one final of a European Championship has been decided by a penalty shoot-out – when Czechoslovakia beat Germany in 1976. What was the penalty shoot-out score? Tick the answer from these options.

3-2 ☑   2-0 ☑   4-3 ☑   5-3 ☑   5-4 ☑

The answer is on page 48.

COACH SPOTLIGHT

The coach of each of the 24 nations competing at UEFA EURO 2020 is just as important as the superstar players. Here you will find out about different coaching styles and the ways in which an international coach influences a match.

WHAT DOES A COACH DO?

The head coach of a team has a vital job. He or she has to pick the 23 players for their squad, and then the 11 who will start each match. The coach also trains the players and gets them ready for games and a tournament.

IS A COACH MORE IMPORTANT THAN THE PLAYERS?

Ultimately it is the players who can score or stop goals, but a coach also has the power to make things happen in a game. The coach can take players off and bring new players on, called a substitution, and tell players to make certain passes and attacking runs.

WHAT ARE TEAM TACTICS?

Tactics refer to a team's approach to a game – for example, attacking or counter-attacking. A team playing in an attacking style try to score lots of goals. A defensive team focus on keeping the ball out of their goal but then counter-attacking by quickly turning defence into attack with a long pass or run from defence. The head coach decides a team's tactics and formation (see pages 30–31).

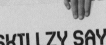

SKILLZY SAYS

At 74 years of age, Giovanni Trapattoni was the oldest coach at EURO 2012.

Currently France's coach, Didier Deschamps holds the trophy as France's captain at EURO 2000.

TM

GARETH SOUTHGATE

The England coach took his team to the 2018 FIFA World Cup semi-final and to the semi-final of the UEFA Nations League in 2019. Southgate is happy to change tactics and team formation depending on the opposition and likes to use quick, attacking players.

ROBERTO MANCINI

The former Italy international has enjoyed success with big club teams like Inter Milan and Manchester City, and now he has the *Azzurri* in championship-winning form once again. His exciting 4-3-3 system is full of goals and features a defence that is tough to break down.

ROBERTO MARTÍNEZ

With versatile and quick-thinking players like Eden Hazard and Kevin De Bruyne in his team, Belgium coach Martínez has a dream job. He fields attacking midfielders to score and relies on the hard work and power of strikers such as Romelu Lukaku and Michy Batshuayi.

JOACHIM LÖW

Germany's head coach is a proven winner of big tournaments. Löw has lifted the 2014 FIFA World Cup and 2017 FIFA Confederations Cup. He was runner-up with Germany at EURO 2008 – 13 years on he is hoping to finally land the prize.

WINNING FORMATIONS

The way a team sets up on the pitch dictates the tactics they might use in a match. Football experts often refer to specific number systems to talk about team formations. Read on to find out how these work.

4-4-2
The 4-4-2 football system is very popular. Most teams use it at some point. The outfield players are made up of four defenders, four midfielders and two strikers. The defenders feature two centre-backs and two full-backs, with two central midfielders and a right- and left-winger.

4-3-3
Playing in a 4-3-3 system makes sense when a team has three forward players and three defensive, yet creative midfielders. Using this formation, a team is likely to create more scoring opportunities. Spain, for example, can play in this way, using Álvaro Morata or Rodrigo as the central striker.

4-2-3-1
Two defensive midfielders help the defenders protect the goal. Three attacking players then support a lone striker. The right players can make the 4-2-3-1 system very effective. England sometimes use this system, with players such as Raheem Sterling, Jordan Sancho and Marcus Rashford linking up with striker Harry Kane up front.

4-5-1
This line-up is a bit more defensive than a normal 4-4-2. The five midfielders offer more protection to stop the opposition attacking. With just one main striker, any chances that are created have to be taken quickly. Poland sometimes play this system, relying on the skills of captain Robert Lewandowski in attack.

England's Harry Kane linking up with Raheem Sterling in a 4-2-3-1 system.

3-5-2
This is another popular system with three centre-backs, five midfielders and two strikers. In practice, though, the five midfielders include a right and left wing-back. The wing-backs attack from wide positions but also have to help in defence. England and Belgium have played like this in recent tournaments.

PICK PLAYERS FOR THE PERFECT SYSTEM

Now that you know about formations, list your favourite 11 UEFA EURO 2020 players in a team formation of your choice. Choose players from any country to create your ultimate dream team!

Attackers

Midfielders

Defenders

Goalkeeper

PLAYER PUZZLES

How good is your knowledge of some of the superstar players who have lit up previous EURO finals with their great performances? It is time to find out!

FOCUS HARD

The match photographer has not focused their camera properly. Can you name each of these players?

1 _____ 2 _____ 3 _____

The answers are at the back of the book.

SUPERSTAR SCRAMBLE

The letters that make up the name of this legendary EURO finals player from the past have been scrambled up. Can you work out who it is?

CLUE: he has won the UEFA Champions League both as a player and coach.

INDIAN ZED ZEE IN

The answers are on page 48.

SPOT THE DIFFERENCE 2

Can you spot the five changes made to picture B of the EURO 2016 final? Circle them all.

A

B

TEN TEST

Can you name each of these star players wearing the No10 shirt?

1

2

3

1 ....

2 ....

3 ....

LINK THE LEGENDS

Can you link these past legends of EURO tournaments to the country they played for.

1

Gianluigi Buffon

2

Alan Shearer

3

Oliver Bierhoff

4

Xabi Alonso

5

Zlatan Ibrahimović

6

Andrey Arshavin

Spain

Sweden

England

Italy

Russia

Germany

PLAYER WATCH: FORWARDS

The next eight pages are jam-packed with the hottest UEFA EURO 2020 stars! To kick things off, here's the lowdown on the most fearsome forwards with a deadly aim in front of goal.

HARRY KANE
Country: England
Club: Tottenham Hotspur
Born: 28 July 1993
Major trophies: 2018 FIFA World Cup Golden Boot

England captain Kane was the team's talisman in his last major international tournament, scoring six goals at the 2018 FIFA World Cup. Having already scored more than 30 international goals, could Kane blast his way to becoming the first English captain to be crowned a European champion in 2021?

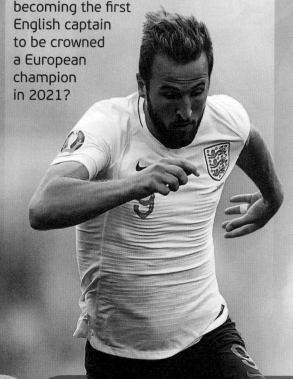

CRISTIANO RONALDO
Country: Portugal
Club: Juventus
Born: 5 February 1985
Major trophies: UEFA EURO 2016, UEFA Nations League 2019, UEFA Champions League

Ronaldo is still one of the top finishers in world football. The Portugal superstar can blast in long-range shots, score with amazing free-kicks and bury penalties. He has incredible strength, speed and ball skills, and leads Portugal's attacks with his classy style of play.

KYLIAN MBAPPÉ
Country: France
Club: Paris Saint-Germain
Born: 20 December 1998
Major trophies: 2018 FIFA World Cup, Ligue 1

France's star striker Mbappé is absolutely lethal in attack! The youngster is a devastating mix of speed, strength and laser-guided shooting. With Mbappé playing alongside the likes of Antoine Griezmann and Olivier Giroud, France could go all the way at EURO 2020.

TIMO WERNER

Country: Germany
Club: Chelsea
Born: 6 March 1996
Major trophies: 2017 FIFA Confederations Cup

Germany have a long history of producing world-class strikers and Werner is the latest to spearhead their attack. He scored ten goals in his first 25 international games, using his sharp skills and natural finishing technique to beat the best goalkeepers. Werner will be a major international force for many years to come.

ROBERT LEWANDOWSKI

Country: Poland
Club: Bayern Munich
Born: 21 August 1988
Major trophies: Bundesliga, UEFA Champions League

With 50+ international goals to his name, Poland's talisman, No1 striker, and captain has a reputation as among the finest strikers in Europe. Lewandowski can hold the ball up, burst into the box and out-jump defenders to score headers. Even though he will turn 33 later this summer, Lewandowski is still a key player.

PLAYER WATCH: MIDFIELDERS

An international midfielder must be able to score, pass, tackle, cross and run for the whole game! There are different types of midfielders, from defensive to attacking and those who play out wide. Check out five of the best midfielders on show at UEFA EURO 2020.

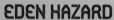

EDEN HAZARD

Country: Belgium
Club: Real Madrid
Born: 7 January 1991
Major trophies: UEFA Europa League, Premier League, La Liga

Every coach at EURO 2020 would welcome a player like Hazard in his team! Belgium's brilliant playmaker is a master at passing and dribbling, losing defenders and breaking into the area to finish a move. With Hazard in their line-up, Belgium pose a threat to any side in the world.

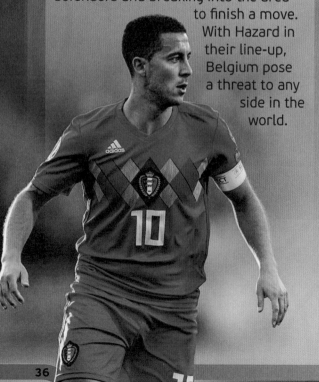

FRENKIE DE JONG

Country: Netherlands
Club: Barcelona
Born: 12 May 1997
Major trophies: Eredivisie

Blessed with so much natural talent, De Jong can play as a defensive midfielder, box-to-box attacker or even a centre-back! He has already proved his class at international level by helping the Netherlands reach the UEFA Nations League final. Could he help his team go one better at EURO 2020?

TONY KROOS

Country: Germany
Club: Real Madrid
Born: 5 January 1990
Major trophies: 2014 FIFA World Cup, UEFA Champions League, La Liga, Bundesliga

Kroos is still the player that drives Germany's midfield, controlling the tempo and setting up his team's pacey forwards. In the EURO 2020 qualifiers he scored three goals in five games to show exactly what he brings to big international games.

SERGIO BUSQUETS

Country: Spain
Club: Barcelona
Born: 16 July 1988
Major trophies: 2010 FIFA World Cup, UEFA EURO 2012, UEFA Champions League, La Liga

The ever-reliable Busquets always does the business for *La Roja*! Although perhaps not a flair player like Spain's Isco and Rodri, the midfield maestro is an expert at reading the game, winning the ball and getting his team on the attack. His international experience is vital in Spain's central midfield.

PAUL POGBA

Country: France
Club: Manchester United
Born: 15 March 1993
Major trophies: 2018 FIFA World Cup, UEFA Europa League, Serie A

Sometimes the opposition finds it impossible to dispossess Pogba – his power, height and quick feet can be mesmerising. As well as bossing the centre of the pitch, the Frenchman has the speed to run into the box and strike the net with a precise shot or header.

PLAYER WATCH: DEFENDERS

A defender's job is to stop the opposition from scoring. Some defenders are tough and ruthless, and others use their speed and footwork to protect their goal. The very best, though, are a combination of these skills!

SERGIO RAMOS
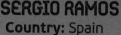
Country: Spain
Club: Real Madrid
Born: 30 March 1986
Major trophies: 2010 FIFA World Cup, UEFA EURO 2008 and 2012, UEFA Champions League, La Liga

Winner of more than 20 club trophies, as well as the FIFA World Cup and two EURO titles, Ramos is no stranger to picking up silverware! He does not give strikers any space in the box and knows when to step forward and tackle or drop back to help his goalkeeper. Awesome at scoring from free-kicks and corners.

LEONARDO BONUCCI

Country: Italy
Club: Juventus
Born: 1 May 1987
Major trophies: Serie A, Coppa Italia, UEFA EURO 2012 runner-up

As a multiple winner of the Italian league title, Bonucci definitely knows what it takes to win major trophies. He has also had disappointment at the EURO final after losing in 2012, so success this year would help make up for that defeat. The experienced centre-back is a master of closing strikers down, dispossessing the opposition and clearing any danger inside his penalty box.

RAPHAËL VARANE
Country: France
Club: Real Madrid
Born: 25 April 1993
Major trophies: 2018 FIFA World Cup, UEFA Champions League, La Liga

Ruled out of France's UEFA EURO 2016 finals because of injury, Varane is desperate to help his side to the title this summer. With his cool mix of strength, tackling, passing and leadership skills, he is the man *Les Bleus* rely on to keep their backline together.

TOBY ALDERWEIRELD

Country: Belgium
Club: Tottenham Hotspur
Born: 2 March 1989
Major trophies: Eredivisie, La Liga, UEFA Champions League runner-up

Alongside the experienced Jan Vertonghen, Alderweireld has formed one of the best centre-back pairings in international football in recent years. He has a solid all-round game, using smart tackles, perfect positioning and strong heading skills to protect his goal.

TRENT ALEXANDER-ARNOLD

Country: England
Club: Liverpool
Born: 7 October 1998
Major trophies: UEFA Champions League, Premier League

The dynamic full-back is the best example of an attacking defender in European football. The youngster has the speed to help his backline but can also burst forward and link up with the midfielders. Alexander-Arnold is a master free-kick taker as well.

PLAYER WATCH: GOALKEEPERS

With a commanding keeper in goal a country always has the chance of picking up wins and points and moving closer to the UEFA EURO 2020 knockout games! Check out the current crop of Europe's greatest goalies.

THIBAUT COURTOIS
Country: Belgium
Club: Real Madrid
Born: 11 May 1992
Major trophies: FIFA Club World Cup, La Liga, Premier League, UEFA Europa League

Courtois already has plenty of experience, notching up around 80 international appearances and winning club trophies in three different countries. His tall and agile frame makes him an imposing figure in goal. He has all the qualities of a top keeper, including alertness, quick reflexes and bravery.

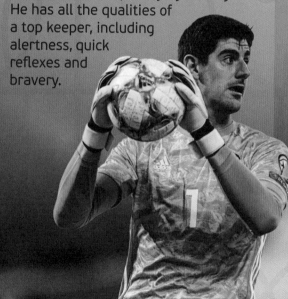

JORDAN PICKFORD
Country: England
Club: Everton
Born: 7 March 1994
Major trophies: UEFA Nations League third place

Pickford might not be the tallest keeper at EURO 2020, but is always quick to race from his line to clear any danger and uses his strong kicks to set up counter-attacks. He will be raring to go in his first EURO finals.

HUGO LLORIS
Country: France
Club: Tottenham Hotspur
Born: 26 December 1986
Major trophies: 2018 FIFA World Cup, UEFA Champions League runner-up

The French captain won the FIFA World Cup in 2018 and now he wants the EURO 2020 title as well! Lloris is a calm presence in goal and bosses his defenders to keep opposition strikers at bay.

MANUEL NEUER

Country: Germany
Club: Bayern Munich
Born: 27 March 1986
Major trophies: 2014 FIFA World Cup, UEFA Champions League, Bundesliga

Germany fans love the sight of Neuer snatching the ball from a striker's feet and launching it down the field! The veteran goalkeeper is famous for his 'sweeper keeper' style, coming out from his area to turn defence into attack. This could be the captain's final chance to win the UEFA EURO trophy.

WOJCIECH SZCZESNY

Country: Poland
Club: Juventus
Born: 18 April 1990
Major trophies: Serie A, FA Cup

Szczesny has suffered suspension and injury problems that have ruled him out of past EURO finals. Now, though, the Juventus star is in the best form of his career and ready to prove why he's so highly rated. West Ham United keeper Łukasz Fabiański presses him for the No1 spot.

THE GROUP STAGE

Who will be crowned champions at UEFA EURO 2020? Use the fill-in charts to follow your team's progress through the competition.

GROUP A TEAM	P	W	D	L	GD	PTS
1						
2						
3						
4						

GROUP B TEAM	P	W	D	L	GD	PTS
1						
2						
3						
4						

GROUP C TEAM	P	W	D	L	GD	PTS
1						
2						
3						
4						

GROUP D

TEAM	P	W	D	L	GD	PTS
1						
2						
3						
4						

GROUP E

TEAM	P	W	D	L	GD	PTS
1						
2						
3						
4						

GROUP F

TEAM	P	W	D	L	GD	PTS
1						
2						
3						
4						

ROUND OF 16

26 JUNE, MATCH 37, **LONDON**

WINNER GROUP A   RUNNERS-UP GROUP C

v

GOALS [ ] [ ] GOALS

SCORERS   SCORERS

26 JUNE, MATCH 38, **AMSTERDAM**

RUNNERS-UP GROUP A   RUNNERS-UP GROUP B

v

GOALS [ ] [ ] GOALS

SCORERS   SCORERS

27 JUNE, MATCH 39, **BILBAO**

WINNER GROUP B   THIRD PLACE GROUP A/D/E/F

v

GOALS [ ] [ ] GOALS

SCORERS   SCORERS

27 JUNE, MATCH 40, **BUDAPEST**

WINNER GROUP C   THIRD PL. GROUP D/E/F

v

GOALS [ ] [ ] GOALS

SCORERS   SCORERS

28 JUNE, MATCH 41, **COPENHAGEN**

RUNNERS-UP GROUP D   RUNNERS-UP GROUP E

v

GOALS [ ] [ ] GOALS

SCORERS   SCORERS

28 JUNE, MATCH 42, **BUCHAREST**

WINNER GROUP F   THIRD PL. GROUP A/B/C

v

GOALS [ ] [ ] GOALS

SCORERS   SCORERS

29 JUNE, MATCH 43, **GLASGOW**

WINNER GROUP E   THIRD PLACE GROUP A/B/C/D

v

GOALS [ ] [ ] GOALS

SCORERS   SCORERS

29 JUNE, MATCH 44, **DUBLIN**

WINNER GROUP D   RUNNERS-UP GROUP F

v

GOALS [ ] [ ] GOALS

SCORERS   SCORERS

QUARTER-FINALS

2 JULY, 18:00 (CET), MATCH 45, **SAINT PETERSBURG**

WINNER MATCH 41	WINNER MATCH 42
v	

GOALS			GOALS
SCORERS			SCORERS

---

2 JULY 21:00 (CET), MATCH 46, **MUNICH**

WINNER MATCH 39	WINNER MATCH 37
v	

GOALS			GOALS
SCORERS			SCORERS

---

3 JULY 18:00 (CET), MATCH 47, **BAKU**

WINNER MATCH 40	WINNER MATCH 38
v	

GOALS			GOALS
SCORERS			SCORERS

---

3 JULY 21:00 (CET), MATCH 48, **ROME**

WINNER MATCH 43	WINNER MATCH 44
v	

GOALS			GOALS
SCORERS			SCORERS

SEMI-FINALS

6 JULY, 21:00 (CET), MATCH 49, **LONDON**

WINNER MATCH 45   WINNER MATCH 46

v

GOALS [ ]   [ ] GOALS

BEST MOMENT OF THE MATCH

SCORERS   SCORERS

7 JULY, 21:00 (CET), MATCH 50, **LONDON**

WINNER MATCH 47   WINNER MATCH 48

v

GOALS [ ]   [ ] GOALS

BEST MOMENT OF THE MATCH

SCORERS   SCORERS

UEFA EURO 2020 FINAL

11 JULY, 21:00 (CET), MATCH 51, **LONDON**

WINNER MATCH 49	WINNER MATCH 50

V

LINE-UP	LINE-UP

SUBSTITUTES	SUBSTITUTES

GOALS			GOALS

SCORERS	SCORERS

MAN OF THE MATCH

BEST MOMENT OF THE MATCH

ANSWERS

Page 7: Winning goals
1C
2A
3B

Page 9: Just 'four' fun
Wales 3-1 Belgium
Czech Republic 2-2 Croatia
Spain 4-0 Republic of Ireland

Page 11: Top team time
Toni Kroos and Cristiano Ronaldo

Page 13: Host watch
Italy, Denmark, Russia, Scotland, Hungary,
Rep of Ireland, Romania, Azerbaijan

Page 19: Pick a card
1. FRA vs IRE: red card
2. POR vs WAL: yellow card

Page 20: Which kit?
1. Netherlands
2. Belgium
3. Italy

Page 20: Code cracker
Portugal

Page 20: Eye know
1. Eden Hazard
2. Harry Kane
3. Robert Lewandowski

Page 20: Kidding around
1. Hugo Lloris
2. Cristiano Ronaldo
3. Álvaro Morata

Page 21: Year we go
1. 2004
2. 2012
3. 2016

Page 23: Spot the ball
A3

Page 25: Spot the difference

Page 27: Shoot-out score
Czechoslovakia 5-3 Germany (2-2 aet)

Page 32: Focus hard
1. Luka Modrić
2. Xherdan Shaqiri
3. Raheem Sterling

Page 32: Superstar scramble
Zinedine Zidane

Page 33: Spot the difference 2

Page 33: Ten test
1. Julian Brandt
2. Granit Xhaka
3. Eden Hazard

Page 33: Link the legends
Gianluigi Buffon – Italy
Alan Shearer – England
Oliver Bierhoff – Germany
Xabi Alonso – Spain
Zlatan Ibrahimović – Sweden
Andrey Arshavin – Russia